Please, Miss Sybil, Don't Give Up!

James Dan Casey

Copyright @ 2025 by James Dan Casey

All Rights Reserved. No part of this publication may be reproduced, distributed, or transmitted in any form or by any means, including photoshopping, recording, or other electronic or mechanical methods without prior written permission of the author and publisher, except in the case of the brief quotations embodied in reviews and certain other noncommercial uses permitted by copyright law. For information regarding permission, email the author at caseyjamesdan@gmail.com

This book is a work of fiction. Names, characters, and incidents, are either the product of the author's imagination or are used fictitiously, and any resemblance to actual persons living or dead, business establishment, events, or locales, is entirely coincidental.

First Edition Book, September, 2025

ISBN 978-1-7375716-8-1 Hardcover
ISBN 978-1-7375716-9-8 Paperback

Book cover design, illustration, editing, and interior layout by:

www.1000storybooks.com

Dedication

I would like to dedicate this book to my daughter, Allison Casey. She has been there as a consultant for me on the readiness of children for various stories. I use her as a sounding board for my story ideas and the age group that would benefit from them. It was Allison's suggestion to write about Sybil Ludington, dubbed the "female Paul Revere." In reality, Miss Sybil rode further and reached more people than Revere ever did. She's an unsung heroine.

Emily and Jake could hardly wait until Saturday to go time traveling. This week, Jake was waiting for Emily. They both had their bikes and Jake dared her, "Let's race!"

Emily was caught off guard and didn't get a good start. Jake won by a bike length. He laughed and pointed at Emily.
"One time, Jake, that's all you get," Emily said.

They ran up the library stairs and hurried back to the closet, jumped on the machine, and hit the button. This time, they landed in the woods with no town around. This was the first time they had not landed in a building.

"I don't like this. How will we get back?" Jake said.
"I don't like it either. It's cold, dark, and raining hard." The air was cold and smelled of wet wood from the branches. It was totally dark and the wind blowing made the branches creak.
"This is spooky. What if we can't find our way out of here, Emily?" Jake moaned.

"Don't think about that. Let's walk this way!" Emily had to shout because the heavy rain was hammering down.
The wind was blowing so hard, they could barely walk forward. Then, Emily saw someone on horseback in the darkness and blinding rain. The rider didn't slow down and waved a big stick as she rode toward them.

They started yelling, "Stop! Stop! We need help!"

"Get out of my way!" The rider shouted.

Emily turned to Jake and shouted, "It's a girl! What could she be doing out here in the middle of a storm?"

"I don't know, but she's coming fast! We better get out of her way."

Emily shouted back to the girl, "We're lost! We don't mean any harm."

As she slowed to a stop beside them, the kids saw that the rider wore a long dress was very young, breathing hard, and leaning down on the horse. Her head was bowed. She looked like she couldn't go any further.

"Well, you shouldn't be out here; the redcoats patrol this area."

The rider shifted a bit. "I don't recognize you. Are you from town?"

"Not really. My name is Emily, and this is Jake."

"I'm Sybil Ludington. The British are burning Danbury. I'm trying to get all the militia from their farms to go report to my father." She leaned closer. "I'm beating on their door with this stick and yelling, 'Call to Arms! Colonel Ludington's house by dawn!'"

As she yelled, her voice cracked. Sybil sighed loudly. She was still leaning over and it seemed she might fall off the horse.

"I've come almost twenty miles so far, and I have twenty more to go. I'm soaked and cold, hungry, and tired. I keep nodding off to sleep on top of my horse."

"Wait—we know who you are," Jake said eagerly.

"Yeah!" Emily joined in. "Our teacher was reading about heroes of the American Revolution. You're only sixteen."

"Well, I'm no hero—wait, how do you know I'm sixteen?"

"We're from the future," Emily said.

"Now, I know I'm dreaming." Sybil shook her head and wiped her face. "I must wake up and keep going. I don't know if I'm going to make it all the way."

"You're awake," Jake said. "We really are from the future. We are time travelers. We visit people in history and try to encourage them. You will make it if you keep trying. We know you will. It's history."

"Thank you." She smiled and sat up a little straighter. "I'll do my best. If you keep walking that direction, you'll come to a town in about two miles." With that, she said good luck and galloped away. They watched her disappear into the darkness.

Emily shouted, "Please, Miss Sybil, don't give up!"

They were both shivering, and it was difficult to walk in the mud. The rain wouldn't stop, they were soaked, and it was so cold. Neither Emily nor Jake had coats. They walked for about five minutes before they heard rustling in the trees. It startled them, and they both looked in that direction.

"It's the redcoats," Jake whispered urgently. "Four of them, on horses!"

"Be quiet," Emily whispered. "They haven't seen us. Let's get behind that tree."

The redcoats were walking their horses really close to them when suddenly Jake sneezed. One of the soldiers turned his horse and peered into the brush. "Halt! Who goes there?"

"Run, Jake, run!" They both took off running as fast as they could. The soldiers turned their horses and rode toward them. The mud was slowing them down. One of the soldiers jumped off his horse and grabbed them both. They struggled but couldn't get away.

"Who are you?" He hesitated. "You're children. What are you doing out here?" He shook them then yelled, "Who were you talking to?" Jake and Emily both began to cry.

"Is General Washington making children spies now?" The soldier spit to the side. "We're taking you to our camp."

"We're not spies!" Emily said.

"Just let us go!" said Jack angrily.

"Not until the captain talks to you."

"You two, ride that way and see if you can catch who they were talking to." He paused for a moment then ordered, "Wait, never mind. It's raining too hard to catch him. We'll get it out of them, anyway."

They made the kids walk in front of them toward their camp. As Emily and Jake walked, they each thought of what could happen to captured spies in war time. They both felt like crying again, but suddenly the ground fell away beneath them, and they began falling in the dark. They didn't know where they would land or even if it would be at their home library. It was a terrible feeling. Thankfully, they landed in their library closet. Strangely, they were dry and warm and the mud was gone. They weren't frightened anymore.

"That was close," Emily said.

"I was scared to death," Jake said. "Wait a minute. How do we know if Miss Sybil made it?"

"When we disappeared, they probably went after her," Emily answered.

"I know. Let's find her in the encyclopedia." They walked over to a bookshelf and found the "L" encyclopedia for Ludington. Jake was flipping pages when Emily got impatient and grabbed the book away from him. Emily began reading silently.

"What does it say?" Jake said impatiently.

"It talks about her father, the Colonel, and the messenger who delivered the bad news about Danbury. Sybil's father didn't know who to send to the farms and gather the militia. It says that Sybil spoke up, saying, "Let me! I can ride as well as any man! Star knows the woods just like I do.' Star must have been her horse's name. It looks like she succeeded! She got away, and warned the militia!"

Jake and Emily looked at each other, eyes wide.

"That's us!" Jake exclaimed. "We did that. We delayed the redcoats long enough for Miss Sybil to get away!"

They both had big smiles and gave each other a high five.

Emily continued, "It says the Colonel and his four hundred men joined up with General Washington's army, surprised the British, and pushed them all the way back to the ships they came in on. It was a huge victory."

"She was a hero," Jake said.

"Heroine, a female hero," Emily corrected him.

"Sybil did it, all on her own. We didn't have to go back to help her."

Cars were speeding back and forth as usual. "They have no idea what we just did!"
Emily said.

"Let's celebrate and get a popsicle," Emily shouted. She stood up on her pedals and went as fast as she could. She was determined that she was going to beat Jake, but also to ride faster than any redcoats that chased Miss Sybil.

Join Emily and Jake on their next adventure to visit Alexander Graham Bell. He is trying to invent the telephone, but he is struggling. Will he give up, or can Emily and Jake convince him to carry on? Our future depends on it. We must have telephones! How else can we call our friends?

www.ingramcontent.com/pod-product-compliance
Lightning Source LLC
LaVergne TN
LVHW071029070426
835507LV00002B/80